The Written Work of My Most Inner Thoughts

Candice Sarangay

BookLeaf
Publishing

Presentation by *BookLeaf Publishing*

Web: www.bookleafpub.com

E-mail: info@bookleafpub.com

ISBN: 9789357745048

First edition 2022

*I dedicate this collection of poetry to my
late dad. Who always supported my dreams
and had my back. May you rest in peace
and read the poems I wrote for you.*

ACKNOWLEDGEMENT

Thank you to my family who always supported my writing!

Thank you to my friends who pushed me into continuing my writing.

Thank you to Bookleaf Publishing for allowing me to participate in the challenge.

And thank you to myself for taking a chance.

PREFACE

Hello everyone that chose to indulge in my poetry. First off, thank you. Thank you for having the desire to read my work. I hope you enjoy reading the thoughts that came from my brain and that are everchanging. I write to live, to be free and to be creative. I hope something in this collection evokes you in any type of way, whether that be for better or worse. It lets me know that you feel something, as I felt many emotions during the writing process. To all the readers, writers, and creative wonders in the world, thank you being alive and keep doing what you do. Creating art for all to see. Thank you for shedding light on a portion of what I like to call, my world and my home. Enjoy!

The Lady in Red

The lady in red
Was she that way because she bled?
Took a spill to the head?
And now is pronounced dead?

She was called that because of her hands
Stained from her work's hectic demands
She loved the day to day routine
But hated contributing to the crime scene

She had to do it, she had no choice
Or risk losing her precious voice
She patiently waited by the phone
In her dark, depressing office...all alone

Her phone lit up with every task
She accepted them all, no need to ask
Say hi to her for me
She's often hard to spot and see

You might miss her if you blink
Because she visits you more than you think.

Obstruction

The block
Big, rectangular, solid
You obstruct my path
And clog my brain

The block
Trapping me within your walls
Choking me with your grasp
Growing more and more by the second

The block

Stop making me stuck
I'm sinking in your quicksand
Flailing around, gasping for air

The block
You inhibit me from being free
To speak, to move, to flow
Let me be me...please

Move your stupid block
You stupid, massive, condescending block

Thanks for Visiting

I saw you last night.

I've been kinda waiting for you
But I know you're busy with other plans
Taking trips to other people

It was nice to see you
Any version of you
You looked the same
How you did in recent years

I guess that's how I remember you
My long term memory is not so good
Are you making your way through the family?
Before you go

I appreciate you finally getting to me
Come over more often
Stop by anytime you're free
I hope I see you again soon

I love you dad.

Thanks for visiting.

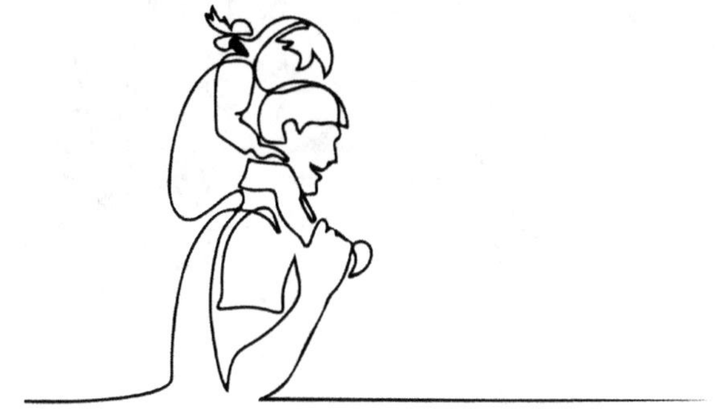

Reflection

I wake up everyday
 Prod and poke my face away
 I sometimes hate the way I look in you
 I wish I could see what you see and step
through

 Into your world and opposite views
 That ever changes like a short fuse
 The portal to your realm is everywhere
 In multiple shapes: triangle, circle, square

My mirror is my captor
I'm its prisoner, waiting to escape in the next
chapter
It distorts my reflection
As I touch my neck and mid-section

But something was off this time
The mirror didn't mimic or mime
It's like it had its own brain and wit
As I stared long and hard into it

It became clearer and clearer
As it asked, so... you're the reflection in the
mirror?

Weather Words

Drip, drip, drip
Rain, rain, rain
Puddle, puddle, puddle
Drip, rain, puddle

Rain, drip, drip, rain
Rain, drip, drip, rain
Drip, puddle, drip
Drip, puddle, drip

Puddle, rain, puddle, puddle
Rain, puddle, rain, rain
Puddle, rain, puddle, puddle
Rain, puddle, rain, rain

Drip, rain, puddle
Puddle, rain, drip
Puddle, rain, drip
Drip, rain, puddle

I don't like rain.
But, I like thunder and lightning.

Lazy Ron

Ron was a real bore
He was lazy and hate to do a chore
There were many to do on the farm
but he had trouble with no arms
Because he was a dinosaur!

Power Outage

It was gone in the blink of an eye
I let out my frustration with a sigh
I bid farewell to my communication...bye
Darkness would soon fill the sky

I was worried about my protection
This building, far from perfection
With its lack of connection
Launched a full investigation

The rain started to pour
The sky letting out a roar
Cold set into the floor
Which spiraled me into a deep bore

The electricity ran dry with no power
Depleting the entire tower
Turning my day sour
As it continued for hours and hours

Gone was the electricity
Which turned my life back to, simplicity

Warmth

Cold wind roaring out
 The last day in February
 Please warm up sooner

Another Sign of You

I enjoyed seeing you again
 Thanks for the relationship advice
I don't remember exactly what you said
Other than, take more chances

You looked different than before
How you looked before your illness
We were in the living room
Sitting and talking

It was a quick trip
So I don't remember it well
But it must have been important
For you to come down and comfort me

Then one of your songs came on the radio
Another sign you were there
Thanks for watching over me
From the big, blue sky

I love and miss you dad
Thanks for visiting again

Tyler the Tortoise

16

Tyler the tortoise lived in a shoe
He loved to go racing, that was true
His competitors always thought he was slow
But he had the means to put on a show
Tyler was super fast, who knew!

Days of the Week

Monday is for work and trying not to snore
Tuesdays are for tacos, guac, and more
Wednesday is the middle child
Thursdays are calm and mild
Fridays are reserved for fun
Saturdays are recovery for your head spun
And Sundays start it all over again!

A Recipe for Disaster

Step one, wash your hands
Remove the filth and dirt
Next, preheat the oven
So it's not as cold as you

Add in the flour
Not that you ever got me any
Mix the divergent sugars together
You used to be as sweet as them

Beat on the eggs
Like how you beated on my fragile ego
Chop up the chocolate
Just like you did to my heart

Combine well
Like we once were
Slide it into the oven and wait
The same way I did every night

And voila, the recipe is finished
Just like our relationship

Butterfly

My delicate wings
 Propel me far through the air
 So that I may fly

Tubby and Precious

In a house lived two cats
 They hated wearing clothes, even hats
 One was loud, while the other quiet
 They were vastly different based on diet
 Because one was skinny and the other, fat

The Storm

I can't go to certain places
 Without thinking of you
 Your absence fills the area
 With empty lies and promises

The park doesn't seem so bright
The ice cream shop melts my heart instead
The theater only plays depressing films
Even my car is flooded with poor memories

Your love swept me
But your hate drowned me
You destroyed my temple
Made me build up my walls

Endless downpours and wind
You were like a storm I wasn't ready for
Calm in the beginning
Then raging in the end

And that's when I realized...
Why hurricanes are named after people

Earth

They came to our planet on a ship
With their distorted faces and iron grip
They enslaved our kind
Our government overthrown and undermined

Everything I knew began to slip away
For THEY, were here to stay
They kept us in cells and cages
Which felt like ages

They picked us off one by one
Threatening us if we tried to run
They dragged my kind behind a locked door
Once it closed, they were gone for sure

No one knew what happened to those who
disappeared
I knew I would next, I feared
What did they want? I thought
I knew I had to escape, but I would be caught

I had to get out and find the rest of my clan
To be with them and free was the plan
They locked us in cages for hours and hours
Only to unlock it and give us food that was sour

More and more began to vanish
I only await the day, THEY would be banished
Days and days went by
Many anxiously waiting to die

As I feared, it was my turn
Everything behind the door I would soon learn
They dragged me through and strapped me to
table
I heard faint voices saying I was ready and
stable

The atmosphere began to blur, so did my vision
As I felt the knife make a small incision
Suddenly, someone grabbed me
I was out and I was free

I plan to travel to their planet, and show them
my worth
To a planet they call...Earth

Resistance

They took everything from me
My planet, my family, my home
I was finally free
Now in a spaceship dome

Traveling to their home base
To show them my worth
To their dying race
Of now no births

They filled me with so much rage
The way they tortured us
And forced my kind into a cage
While they just sat back and discuss

The human race is abysmal
Greedy, murderous creatures
Whose only world events are cataclysmal
Turning them ugly with grotesque features

They don't know who they're messing with
My planet is strong
We are no lie, rumor, myth
They must finally be proven wrong

We near their planet's star system
It's so dark here
What ravaged their ecosystem?
And turned their planet into a dying sphere

Earth is dying
The humans are the disease
They're not even trying
To save their home from the death squeeze

What is wrong with their kind?
Why didn't they ask for assistance?
Instead of letting their home become misaligned
And be on the brink of extinction

My planet could of done something
But no, they wanted to do it alone
Prove they can do it in one full swing
And let their home turned into a giant pile of
bones

I pity Earth
If only the humans upheld it, with more worth

Chosen

I have searched far and wide
Across many oceans and tides
Searching for the one
To come and end this eternal sun

I have hunted across many moons
Jumping and leaping across sand dunes
The chosen one is close, I can feel it
I will keep going, I will not quit

No longer shall our world be under her rule
People imprisoned and used as tools
I lead the rebellion against her control
And keep fighting until our world is whole

The chosen one is supposed to fix this mess
And be there for us in these times of distress
But alas, they are nowhere to be found
Not a whisper, not a sound

I'm at the end of the map
An old temple, an illusion of a trap
Faint sounds I could hear
Apparently, the chosen one had been gone for
years

There lied in the middle of the floor
The weapon I must bore
The destiny sword
Wielded by the chosen one, as told by the great
wizard lord

The temple collapsed and I was out
I was the new chosen one, I had no doubt
Strong and powerful I stood
I must destroy her once and for good

I hear the cries from my clan and screams from
all
I grab my sword, and take the call

My Guilt

I blame you
 I blame you for my feelings toward sickness
 I blame you for the reason why I hate taking
medicine
 I blame you for the reason why I can't swallow
a damn pill to save my life

 I blame you for making me turn to home
remedies instead of actual medicine that will
cure me faster
 I blame you for the way sickness comes so
easily to you
 I blame you for making me wake up early to
drive you to treatment
 I blame you for making mom cry

 I blame you for putting mom through years of
hardship
 I blame you for making me feel and say these
things

I blame you for somewhat severing our
relationship

I blame you.

My Sorrow

I'm sorry
 I'm sorry for not being there for you
 I'm sorry for not understanding what it must be
like to live with no kidneys
 I'm sorry for the pain you feel

 I'm sorry for not being the best daughter to you
 I'm sorry for not calling more
 I'm sorry I make you think I care more about
mom than I do for you
 I'm sorry I left town for school and couldn't be
there when you needed

 I'm sorry.

Thank You

Thank you

 Thank you for always being there when you
could
 Thank you for not letting me see you cry
 Thank you for sparing more pain I might feel
 Thank you for being my dad

Thank you.